MW01706648

Great Apes

Published by Wildlife Education, Ltd.
12233 Thatcher Court, Poway, California 92064
contact us at: **1-800-477-5034**
e-mail us at: **animals@zoobooks.com**
visit us at: **www.zoobooks.com**

Concept Developed by KIDesign. Scientific Consultant: Mark Rosenthal, Curator Emeritus, Lincoln Park Zoo, Chicago, IL.
Photos: Cover orangutan, Tim Flach (Stone); Half-Title gorilla, Creatas; Title orangutan, Creatas; p. 4, top and bottom, Photodisk/Getty; p. 5, top left, Steve Bloom Images (Alamy); p. 5, bottom left, Photodisk/Getty; p. 5, bottom right, Creatas; pp. 8–9, all photos, Photodisk/Getty; pp. 10-11, Akira Kaede (Photodisc Green); p. 12, gorillas, Creatas; p. 12, inset, Photodisk/Getty; p. 13, orangutans, Photodisk/Getty; p. 14, top, Michael Nichols (National Geographic Image Collection); p. 14, bottom left and middle, Photodisk/Getty; p. 14, bottom right, Creatas.

Copyright © 2005 hardbound edition by Wildlife Education, Ltd.
All rights reserved. No part of this book may be reproduced in any form without written permission from the publisher.
Printed in the U.S.A.

Library of Congress Cataloging-in-Publication Data
Great apes.
p. cm.
ISBN 1-932396-08-X (hardcover)
1. Apes–Juvenile literature. I. Wildlife Education, Ltd.
QL737.P96G732 2005
599.88—dc22

2005012581

Great Apes

Zootles™

big hairy intelligent curious

Aa

Great and *Apes* both make a "long a" sound, like the letter "a." Look for other "long a" sounds throughout this book.

playful great apes!

4 There are **4** apes in this photo. Can you count them?

4 Great Apes

There are many kinds of apes, but the 4 largest are called the great apes.

Gorillas can be huge! Some gorillas weigh as much as **4** grown-up people. Gorillas do climb into trees, but they spend more time on the ground than the other apes do.

Chimpanzees are *very* playful. All chimpanzees, even grown-ups, are smaller than humans, but much, much stronger.

Bonobos are related to chimpanzees, but are a little smaller and often have darker faces. Some people think bonobos are the smartest of the great apes.

Orangutans spend lots of time swinging through the trees. They are easy to recognize by their fluffy, orange hair.

Hey, what about monkeys?

Monkeys are different from apes. One way to tell the difference is that monkeys have tails and apes do not.

For more information on the different kinds of great apes, check out the *Zootles* Resource Corner on p. 22–23.

Welcome to the Rain Forest!

Gorillas, chimpanzees, and **bonobos** live in Africa. **Orangutans** live in Asia. But all great apes live in rain forests!

Great apes love to eat fruits, leaves, berries, flowers, nuts, and even insects! They get water by drinking the rain that collects on leaves.

illustrations by Chris Mills

Most great apes spend lots of time in the trees—swinging, playing, sleeping, and eating.

Great apes are great climbers! They climb and swing to get from place to place, and sometimes just for fun!

4

There are 4 bonobos in this picture. Can you also find 4 birds, 4 flowers, 4 bananas, and 4 tree frogs?

Do great apes just hang around?

Sometimes. But great ape also spend a lot of time looking for food. This chimpanzee i using a long piece of gras to catch insects Yum!

An Ape's Life

Do great apes talk to one another?

No. Great apes don't talk, but they do use sounds, body language, and facial expressions to communicate with one another and show how they feel.

All 4 of the great apes are shown on these two pages

Do great apes live alone?

No. Most great apes live with their families, and ape mothers spend lots of time taking care of their babies.

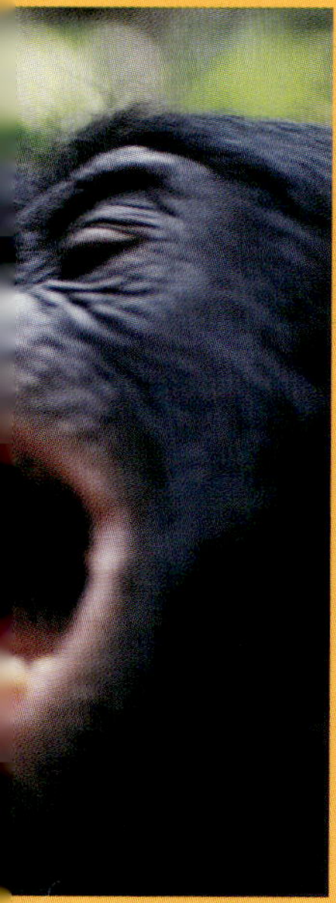

o you know who's who? Go to the *Zootles* Resource Corner on p. 22–23 to find out.

Ape Baby

Ape baby, ape baby,
Where do you play?
In the green and leafy treetops,
Anywhere I may.

Ape baby, ape baby,
How do you play?
Leaping through the forest,
I swing and leap and sway.

Ape baby, ape baby,
When do you play?
Morning, noon, and afternoon,
I play, play, play all day!

by Pavel Mays

Aa

How many times do you hear the word "ape" in the poem "Ape Baby"?

Hands or Feet?

Hands that Walk!

Sometimes great apes walk on two feet, just the way you do. But most of the time, great apes bend over and walk on their feet *and* hands!

Two or four?

Great apes can run faster on all fours than they can on just their two feet. Look at this chimpanzee go!

Strong hands and feet help great apes climb and swing. Look how these orangutans use their hands and feet to grab onto vines and tree branches.

Feet that Grab!

Apes are lucky: they have thumbs on both their hands *and* their feet. These thumbs allow apes to scratch, point, dig, hold, open, close, and even pick things up with their feet!

Hand or foot?

Because it has a thumb, an ape's **foot** looks a lot like a human hand!

Into the Wild

Wildlife scientists like Jane Goodall learn by observing. Dr. Goodall discovered a lot about chimpanzees just by watching and listening.

Many of the things people know about chimpanzees today are things we learned from Jane Goodall.

Jane Goodall learned that chimpanzees

use tools,

have strong family bonds,

and love to play!

You Can Be a Scientist, Too!

Jane Goodall studied chimpanzees in Africa, but you don't have to go to Africa to be a wildlife observer. Use your eyes and ears to learn about animals where *you* live.

A magnifying glass helps you see things that are very small.

Binoculars help you see things that are far away.

What animals can you see in your neighborhood?

Kimo Builds a Night Nest

by Susan Yoder Ackerman

The sun is low in the blue sky. Deep in the ferns and vines of the African rain forest, a gorilla family is finishing its evening meal. Kimo nibbles a last bit of tree bark and then jumps over a mossy log to chase his playmate Nyota.

Kimo's father peels a stalk of wild celery and eats the tender inside. Nyota scampers up his hairy black arm and across his broad silver back. Kimo follows until . . . *whoop*! His father picks Kimo up with one hand and dangles him playfully over his head. Then he sends Kimo scampering and squealing after Nyota.

As Kimo runs by, his mother, Singa, reaches out to stop him. The sun has slipped behind a high mountain peak, and it's time for the gorillas to make their night nests.

Kimo's fingers hold tight to the thick dark hair on his mother's back as she chooses a tree and begins to climb. Up through the low, spreading limbs she goes.

Not far from the ground, Singa finds the perfect spot. Her long arm reaches for a branch, bending it back and tucking it under her. She pulls another branch from the other side, then another and another until they form a springy bed for the two gorillas. She stuffs leaves and twigs between the branches until the nest is the shape of a big green bathtub. In a tree nearby, Nyota is helping her mother with their nest.

Kimo lets go of his mother's back and pulls on a hanging vine, trying to poke it between the branches the way his mother does. The vine falls around his ears and tickles his nose. When Kimo squeals in surprise, Singa pulls the vine off, and then helps him tuck it into a hole to keep out the cold night air.

Singa settles herself into the nest and pulls Kimo close. It's dark now, and the mountain is wrapped in a cold mist, but Kimo is warm and safe. He snuggles against his mother and goes to sleep.

The Adventures of Otto and Allie

story and art by Meg McLean

Zootles Resource Corner

4

The number **4** is featured throughout *Great Apes*. Counting to four, finding fours, identifying sets of four, and learning to connect symbols with numerical concepts is great practice for growing children who are learning their numbers and early math skills. How many **4**s and groups of **4** can you and your child locate together throughout the book?

Aa

Great Apes features the "long a" sound (ā). Learning to identify letters and phonemes is key to developing early reading skills. Long vowels are easy to find—they're the vowels that say their names, as "*a*" does in *ape*. But lots of other letter combinations say the "long a" sound, too, such as *great, way, maid,* or even *neighbor*. How many "long a" sounds can you and your child hear when you read the book together?

Who's WHO?

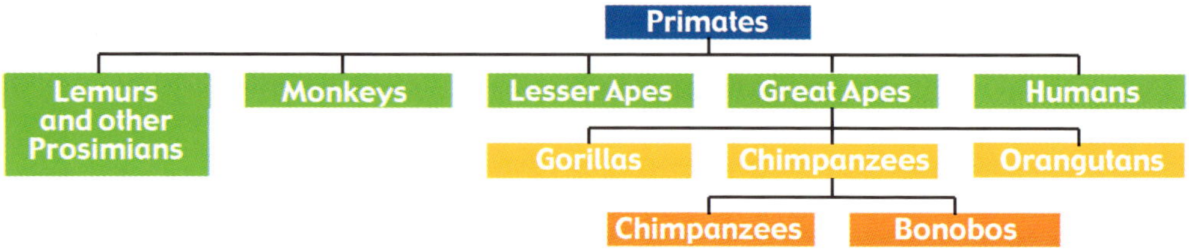

Reading Resource

Every book in the *Zootles* series is designed to be used for fun and learning, and as a reading resource as well. The pages are written simply and address various stages of emerging literacy, and they encourage new readers to exercise their new skills at just the right level. Reading the book together will provide "together time" for you and your child—and reinforce vocabulary, comprehension, and early reading skills, too.

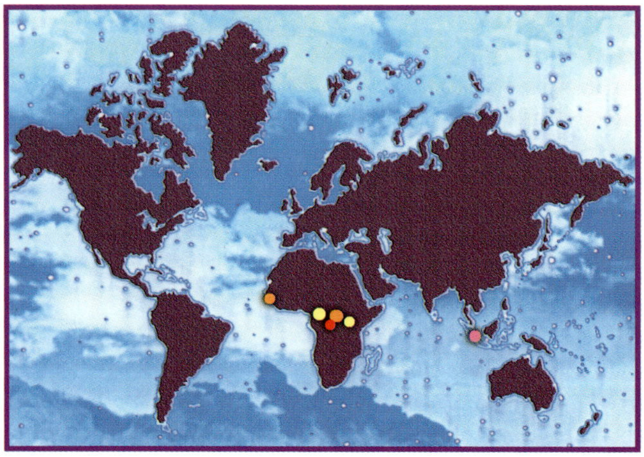

Where in the WORLD?

- **Chimpanzees**
- **Bonobos**
- **Gorillas**
- **Orangutans**

It's a ZOO out there!

Great apes can be fun to watch. If you're fortunate enough to live near a zoo that has a spacious, humane ape habitat, your family may enjoy a trip there after reading *Great Apes*. You'll reinforce learning and encourage careful observation if you look for the ape characteristics and behaviors mentioned in this book:

- toes on the apes' feet
- playing, sleeping, climbing, and looking for food
- walking on two feet or all fours
- communicating with faces, sounds, or body language

How did YOU do? (p. 8-9)

Clockwise from top left: chimpanzee, orangutan mother and baby, young chimpanzee, orangutan, young bonobos, gorilla

What ELSE can we DO?

• **Family Bonding (p. 20)** Ape families spend a lot of time together, and grooming is an important part of their social structure. In "The Adventures of Otto and Allie," Otto and Allie watch chimpanzees groom one another, and then try it for themselves.

- **ZOOTLES TO-DO:** Cut out several small pieces of construction paper and tape them to your shirts or sweaters. Then pretend they are bugs and dirt, and have fun picking them off of one another! Among great apes, grooming reinforces family bonds—it's sure to bring some fun to your house, too!

• **Treetop Sleep (p. 16-19)** In "Kimo Builds a Night Nest,"a young gorilla learns to build a sleeping nest.

- **ZOOTLES TO-DO:** Gather some blankets and pillows and build your own night nest! Then climb in, like Kimo and Singa, and read the story together.

• **Be a Backyard Scientist! (p. 15)** Grab some binoculars, a camera, or a magnifying glass and head out to a natural area near your home.

- **ZOOTLES TO-DO:** Practice good observation skills together: sit still, keep very quiet, listen closely, and always observe wildlife from a safe distance.

• **Gone Fishing! (p. 8)** In the photograph on p.8, a chimpanzee is using a long piece of grass to pull insects from a termite mound.

- **ZOOTLES TO-DO:** Put some raisins or nuts in a glass or cup, dip a drinking straw in honey, and use your "insect-catching stick" to catch and eat some "insects"!

• **Going Ape (p. 12)** Gorillas do most of their walking on all fours, as shown on page 12.

- **ZOOTLES TO-DO:** Imitate the gorilla's knuckle-walk. Most apes move more quickly on all fours than they do on two feet—how quickly can *you* go?

• **Thiiiiiiiiiis Big!** Great apes' arms are longer than their legs.

- **ZOOTLES TO-DO:** Ask your child which he thinks are longer, his arms or his legs. Then measure them to find out!

• **Thiiiiiiiiiis Big! (part 2)** Great apes also have very big hands. An adult male gorilla's hand could be 12 inches long, 7 inches wide, and even hold a basketball!

- **ZOOTLES TO-DO:** Trace your child's hands on a piece of paper, and then measure them from wrist to fingertips and across the palm. How much smaller is your child's hand than a gorilla's?

• **Ape Treats (p. 6)** Many of the foods we eat every day come from the rain forest.

- **ZOOTLES TO-DO:** Gather some rain forest groceries (in this case, bananas, chocolate, coconut, and cinnamon) to make your own ape treats! First, melt a square of semi-sweet chocolate. Then slice a banana lengthwise and spread the melted chocolate on the flat side. Sprinkle with coconut and cinnamon before the chocolate cools, and enjoy!

• **Neat Feet (p. 13)** Great apes have thumbs on their feet, and can use them to climb, hold things, and even pick things up.

- **ZOOTLES TO-DO:** Using a bucket and 6 blocks, take turns trying to pick up the blocks with your feet and put them into the bucket.

• **What Did You Say? (p. 8)** Great apes don't talk to one another, but they do communicate in lots of non-verbal ways.

- **ZOOTLES TO-DO:** Explore body language you can use to tell one another "I'm hungry," "I'm happy," or "I missed you!" Then take turns sending other non-verbal messages to one another and guessing what they mean.

• **Do You See What I See? (p. 15)** Both "You Can Be a Scientist, Too!" and "The Adventures of Otto and Allie" show people using binoculars.

- **ZOOTLES TO-DO:** Find a pair of binoculars and head outside. Introduce your child to the way binoculars work, including magnification and focus. Take a closer look at some neighborhood birds and squirrels!